SUITE HEBRAIQUE

for

Viola (or Violin) and Piano

I. Rapsodie
II. Processional
III. Affirmation

by

Ernest Bloch

G. SCHIRMER, *Inc.*

DISTRIBUTED BY

To the Covenant Club of Illinois

Suite Hébraïque
for Viola (or Violin) and Piano

Ernest Bloch

I. Rapsodie

*Orchestral material available on rental from the publisher.

VIOLIN

G. SCHIRMER, *Inc.*

DISTRIBUTED BY

HAL•LEONARD®
CORPORATION
7777 W. BLUEMOUND RD. P.O. BOX 13819 MILWAUKEE, WI 53213

Suite Hébraïque
for Viola (or Violin) and Piano

Violin

Ernest Bloch

I. Rapsodie

II. Processional

III. Affirmation

Violin

VIOLA

G. SCHIRMER, *Inc.*

DISTRIBUTED BY

HAL•LEONARD®
CORPORATION

7777 W. BLUEMOUND RD. P.O. BOX 13819 MILWAUKEE, WI 53213

To the Covenant Club of Illinois

Suite Hébraïque
for Viola (or Violin) and Piano

Ernest Bloch

I. Rapsodie

Viola

Viola

II. Processional

Andante con moto ♩ = 80

III. Affirmation

Viola

II. Processional

10

III. Affirmation

Maestoso ♩ = 72

U.S. $17.99

ISBN 978-0-7935-5188-0

HL50286080

G. SCHIRMER, Inc.

DISTRIBUTED BY
HAL•LEONARD®

9 780793 551880